It is an honor for me to endor Rodgers. This book will encourage and strengthen all who experience it. Susan not only shares the most difficult times in the life of one of God's most anointed vessels, but tracks the journey she had to endure to survive it. Although the book is entitled *Hidden Scars*, Susan is transparent in her delivery and dynamic in her God-inspired revelations of how to overcome the hurt and pain that lead to ministry and servitude. Women all over the world will rejoice to know all things really do work together for the good of those who love and trust in God. As you read this book, you will discover her pain is real, her devotion to ministry is evident, and her love of God is unsurpassed.

—TERRY MARR, BSN, MSN, MHA
PASTOR, NEW LIFE COMMUNITY CHURCH
MEMPHIS, TENNESSEE

Susan Rodgers is a daughter in the Lord whom I hold in high esteem. As the Lord healed her heart, she has used the healing to help both men and women. Susan loves the Lord and loves God's people and wants the very best for the people of God. Her writing will bless anyone who reads it.

—LORENZO KELLY
JURISDICTIONAL BISHOP, SOUTH DAKOTA
CHURCHES OF GOD IN CHRIST

My wife endured the horrible act and subsequent effects of molestation for many years, but instead of becoming stuck and bitter, she made the decision to seek deliverance. I witnessed the Holy Spirit lead and guide her down the path of deliverance. Susan then made the awesome decision to obey God and share her story of *Hidden Scars*. Though it's common now, it was not common twenty years ago when she started sharing her story in order to help others. I know that this book will help and minister to everyone who reads it, everyone who thought it only happened to them, and everyone that has hidden scars.

Susan and I have served in ministry together since the late Eighties. I know that she loves God and His people. I am blessed to call her my wife and those who read *Hidden Scars* will be blessed that she's an author.

—ADRIAN R. RODGERS
PASTOR, FULLNESS OF JOY AND
NEW DIMENSIONS MINISTRIES

SUSAN RODGERS

HIDDEN SCARS

CREATION
HOUSE

HIDDEN SCARS by Susan Rodgers
Published by Creation House
A Charisma Media Company
600 Rinehart Road
Lake Mary, Florida 32746
www.charismamedia.com

Unless otherwise noted, all Scripture quotations are from the King James Version of the Bible.

Scripture quotations marked AMP are from the Amplified Bible. Old Testament copyright © 1965, 1987 by the Zondervan Corporation. The Amplified New Testament copyright © 1954, 1958, 1987 by the Lockman Foundation. Used by permission.

Scripture quotations marked THE MESSAGE are from *The Message: The Bible in Contemporary English*, copyright © 1993, 1994, 1995, 1996, 2000, 2001, 2002. Used by permission of NavPress Publishing Group.

Design Director: Bill Johnson
Cover design by Nancy Panaccione

Visit the author's websites: fojministries.org and newdministries.org

Library of Congress Cataloging-in-Publication Data: 2011942170
International Standard Book Number: 978-1-61638-820-1
E-book International Standard Book Number: 978-1-61638-821-8

12 13 14 15 16 — 9 8 7 6 5 4 3 2
Printed in the United States of America

DEDICATION

This book is dedicated to my mother, Helen Mildred Russell, a beautiful, intelligent woman whose strength and nurturing gave her children the courage to dream, to love, and to try.

To my husband, Adrian R. Rodgers, you are my soul mate and best friend. Your love is the fulfillment of my childhood dreams. You loved me, believed in me, supported and nurtured me while my scars healed. You are a gift from God!

To my children, Adrian Charles and Brianna, you are a blessing to my life. You both have grown into such intelligent, talented and responsible adults that my heart is full of pride and thanksgiving. I love you both more than you will ever know.

To my brothers and sisters, I love and appreciate you all for your many different gifts and strengths.

To the covenant partners of Fullness of Joy and New Dimensions, you are my extended family. Thank you for loving and believing in me. You have cried with me and rejoiced with me. I can't wait until we all see the vision unfold together.

To my beloved father, the late Johnny Kearney, thank you for pursuing me with fervent love in my adulthood. Your persistence healed a childhood scar and taught me the blessing of a father's love.

ACKNOWLEDGMENTS

I WOULD LIKE TO give special thanks and love to my spiritual father, Bishop Lorenzo Kelly. His fatherly tenderness and prophetic direction brought focus to my scattered soul. He saw value in me before I could see it myself.

I would like to thank and honor Bishop Charles Rodgers. His teaching and passion for excellence gave me a foundation that can never be shaken.

Thanks to Pastor Lenard Hardaway, who taught me to love the Word of God when I was just a teenager.

TABLE *of* CONTENTS

PREFACE

THE WRITING OF this book is a mandate from God. It is the one thing that has been prophesied to me more times that I can remember by perfect strangers. It has been hard for me to write because it has forced me to put into black and white the most difficult journey of my life. But if sharing my story can help anyone find healing or purpose, then I gladly sow the story of my life, my struggles, my mistakes, and my triumphs.

So many people have courageously shared their painful stories of abuse. There are so many awesome books, teachers, and counselors that I hesitate to tell my own story. But I feel called to share it. In many respects, as many popular preachers have said, "My mess has become my message." What the enemy sent to destroy me, God has taken and used to set captives free. This is not a book that bewails the sinful and physical crimes that were committed against me as much as it is about the amazing deliverance that God has manifested in my life over the years. By "deliverance" I don't mean an overnight process by which all the strongholds and demons of my life were exorcized, but rather the process of the Holy Spirit revealing mental and emotional scars left in my soul by the trauma of my past. This process also included the acceptance of God's Word as my truth, the casting down of my old thoughts, speech and lifestyle; and the intentional, progressive application of that truth daily in my mind and in my mouth, which changed my life forever. The process still continues. The more I help others, the more I am helped.

The term *hidden scars* developed when the Holy Spirit began to reveal to me all of the emotional and physical baggage that I was carrying as a result of the trauma of my childhood. Many of us are aware that we have "scars" but we don't always understand how our present scars are connected to our past. We think our "scars" are who we are, not understanding that many of them materialized when we were victimized, abandoned or rejected. Maybe molesters don't realize that the damage they do in the life of a child is so much more than physical. The trauma is not over at the end of the physical act; it is only just beginning.

INTRODUCTION

Y NO MEANS do I belittle the experience of being sexually molested; no one who ever lived through it would do so. I know better than anyone the damage that was done to me. I wish that the physical trauma of molestation and rape were all that there was, that the pain ended at that level. But I came to understand the deep and hidden damage that wounded my soul by the teaching of the Holy Spirit. He has revealed it in the past and is still revealing it to me. But He does not reveal my scars so that I can nurse them; He reveals them so that I can allow Him to begin the healing process—and I do mean process! As much as we understand that it takes time for physical wounds to heal, I don't know why it seems strange to us that emotional scars also need time.

Any kind of abuse (sexual, verbal, physical, emotional), any kind of neglect, abandonment, rejection, or any combination of those against an individual is painful, shameful, and breaks the heart of God. It does not matter how frequently or infrequently it happened. It was wrong. It was sinful. It wounded us. It stole from us. But Christ vindicated our pain. He did not force us to ignore or suppress it but He did ask us to bring it to Him:

> Come unto me, all ye that labor and are heavy laden, and I will give you rest.
> —MATTHEW 11:28

For many of us, childhood trauma stole our self-confidence. Children usually think that they are responsible for what goes

1

on around them, causing them to wonder what it is about them that attracted such behavior. They therefore blame themselves, and their hatred is internalized. This sometimes causes them to mistreat themselves in ways they do not even understand. Abuse steals the sense of adventure that allows most children to pursue life with vigor and abandon. Instead they approach life with fear, caution and mistrust.

It steals from them that innocent sense of trust that would have helped them reach out to others and build healthy relationships. Instead, they isolate themselves and hide. Some hide in crowds, pretending to be the life of the party, all the while feeling disconnected. These victims of abuse only let people get as close as they are comfortable with. Some open themselves up, but only to repeated abusive relationships, because violence and drama are the only ways they know to experience their damaged interpretation of "love."

Many of us bear our wounds in so much shame that it takes years to even mention what happened to us. Some never do. They carry the entire burden of guilt and needless shame all alone. Their mind becomes their biggest battleground as the enemy of their soul accuses and abuses their worth and potential. Their silence gives the enemy an unchallenged voice and opportunity to steal, kill, and destroy. We must learn to speak up! Our silence allows the pain to continue. When we "tell our secret" to someone safe, trustworthy, and non-judgmental, we free ourselves from the burden and shame. We learn to place the guilt where it belongs.

＞◯＜

I pray that there will be a safe, trustworthy adult with whom each wounded child will feel comfortable enough to share his or her pain. We must make the effort to be there for the child in need. We must refuse to turn our heads when we observe danger signals—depressed, bruised, and overly shy children, and children who are more sexually advanced than they should be for their age. We must be the "Good Samaritans" who care more about the wounded than our own inconvenience. It is repeated in the Gospels, "Suffer little children to come unto me, and forbid them not: for such is the kingdom of [heaven]" (Luke 18:16). Children are important to Jesus. They must be important to us also. Children need to know that they have the right to speak up for themselves. We must protect those who cannot protect themselves.

It is so important that they know there is healing for them. I have ministered to hundreds of good Christian people who did not yet understand that Christ offered healing and redemption for their childhood shame. God is the only One who is able to stand in the present, speak to our past, and redeem our future. In Joel 2:25 He says, "I will restore to you the years that the locust hath eaten, the cankerworm, and the caterpillar, and the palmerworm…" The actual text of that scripture has to do with God's restoration of Israel after their repentance from rebellion. But, for our purposes we glean the concept of God being able to "make up" years that we lost due to our affliction and pain.

Too many churches and church leaders feel ill-equipped to deal with the ugly realities that so many children and youths have to face daily. Their loyalties are often divided between helping the parishioner and helping the child. Sometimes the worth of a child's life is lost amid grown-up worries over scandal, marriage, and loss of friendship and membership.

Too often we stand aside and ignore the signs of abuse, opting to turn our heads rather than deal with the truth. Many have told me stories of telling respected Christian adults about their abuse and getting nothing in return—no sympathy, no protection, no embrace, no help. I don't believe it was because those adults did not care; I believe it was because they did not know what to do. This seemingly apathetic response makes the child feel abandoned and allows the abuse to go unchecked.

The subject is ugly. It is uncomfortable. But it is a fact that must be confronted so that these children can have a fighting chance, and so their own children won't see the cycle continue.

Chapter 1

MY STORY

I AM A STATISTIC. My story is like so many of yours; I was sexually molested as a child. I told no one but cousins who were even younger than I was and therefore could do nothing to help me. I was so young when I was molested that I didn't even understand what had happened. I did not cry or scream. I just accepted it. I was raised to respect adults, so I had no idea at the time that an adult could do wrong. I was molested by relatives several times during my childhood. As I got older, all that I was sure of was that I did not like it. It was painful. It felt shameful and filthy. I felt as if I was forced to obey adults and that I could do nothing about it. Most black parents in our area did not discuss these kinds of things with their children back then—at least mine didn't. The circumstances of my life had taught me to blend into the background. "Children should be seen and not heard." "Don't get into grown folks' conversations." I did not know that I could speak up for myself, or tell anyone who would defend me. I thought that I'd get into trouble. So I kept silent.

I don't have many memories of my early childhood. My mother left my father when I was a toddler. The only early memories I have of him are of the stiff, uncomfortable visitations I had as a child. I only saw him once or twice a year, so he felt like a stranger to me. (Our relationship was healed in my adulthood. Thank God!)

My siblings and I were raised by our grandmother for several years while our mother was living and working in another city. Even though I don't remember the specifics of that time, I still remember the feelings of loneliness and abandonment. When Momma came home, I worshiped her more than I loved her. She was like some distant, beautiful goddess to me. I was more afraid of her than close to her because she was such a perfectionist. She had incredibly high standards for us even though we were children. Her stern, sharp corrections did not lend themselves to sharing secrets or confidences. So I kept silent.

The only unconditional love I remember is that of my grandmother. She was small, round, and funny. She played with us. She danced and sang with us. She let us help her in the kitchen. Laughter filled the house whenever she was around. Her love fills up my best childhood memories. I felt completely safe with her, but feeling so small and insignificant in such a busy, large family of which I was the youngest at the time, still I kept silent. Over the years circumstances changed. We moved away from the family that abused me, and I put that part of my life away. I blossomed a little. I became outgoing at school, and gained friends. Puberty was overly generous to me. I became popular. My childhood sexual abuse became only a distant memory; I hardly knew whether it was real or imagined. So I moved on with my life. Even though I battled lots of emotional pain and sadness, I never knew why. I had no clue that my depression and constant loneliness had anything to do with my past; I just thought something was wrong with me.

I became somewhat of an overachiever in school. I do not have a particularly high IQ, but I worked hard to excel in every class that I could to try to gain my mother's approval. I seemed outgoing. I was a cheerleader, majorette, dancer, and public speaker, among other things. Inside though, I was always sick with fear because no matter how much praise I received, all I could seem to concentrate on was the voice inside my head that said I never measured up. This voice said that I had too many things against me to ever really have any worth. I learned to talk tough and act fearless. I pretended to be self-assured, but at every moment I felt that someone was watching me who could see through the facade and had me totally pegged as the frightened little girl that I was.

At the age of fourteen I accepted Christ as my Savior! I knew I'd found the love of my life. I threw everything into my relationship with Christ. His love filled me up all throughout high school. I didn't feel that I needed anyone or anything else. I hid in His love. The world was a distraction for me. All I dreamed of was going to be with Jesus. I lost all sense of ambition for career or material possessions, Christ alone was quite enough! But as time went on, the sadness, loneliness, and fear began to catch up with me again.

During my sophomore year at college, I fell in love with my best friend. He was everything I was not. He was self-confident and outgoing; I had become shy and retiring. He was impetuous and completely without fear; I was cautious and terrified of life. It seemed that my depression gained strength as time passed. His strength made me feel safe. His love was the stuff of storybooks. I didn't know that men could love deeply and purely as he did. We got married in my senior year, and I threw all my strength into being his wife. He was a good place to hide. I didn't have to face my fears and confront my issues. He loved me and protected me from the big, scary world.

It seemed as though my husband had been created just for me. He was confident and fearless enough to protect me completely, yet tender and patient enough to deal with all my issues. He was my hero and loved being so, although I'm sure that as time went on, it became a burden. He told me later that it was overwhelming to have all of someone's hope placed in him. He felt pressured because he was afraid of letting me down. I had grown to be just as hard on the people I loved as I was on myself. My expectations were unrealistic, which made disappointment inevitable. I became increasingly dependent and emotional. I often say that I began to experience depression before it was popular. I only learned what it was in retrospect. At the time, all I knew was that sadness and hopelessness seemed to be taking over my life, and I had no idea how to fight it—and I did so want to fight it!

I graduated from university cum laude and was offered a graduate school scholarship, but I was afraid to take it. I didn't want to go out into the world; I wanted to hide in my home where it was safe. I applied for a few jobs, but nothing came through. I was glad. My fear was a problem because we were struggling financially, and everyone (especially my in-laws) wanted to know why I didn't get a job and help out. How could I explain to them what I did not completely understand myself?

On the outside I looked capable and qualified to obtain a good job, even a lucrative career. But inside I was a frightened child who felt inadequate and desperately afraid of everything. I felt like the "great pretender." I had learned to put on a tough, polished exterior while inside I was falling apart. The criticism of some of my in-laws, though it hurt deeply, was actually in the sovereign will of God because it forced me to begin to face myself. I had never allowed myself to speak of the inner turmoil that I was experiencing except to my one confidante, my husband, who loved me so deeply that he covered me. But confrontation made me admit to myself that my hidden fears were crippling my life. I did not have the courage to do anything about it yet. I wouldn't have known what to do if I had. After two years of marriage, I got pregnant. I'd found another place hide, a little life that I could throw myself into and who would love me unconditionally. A baby wouldn't know that I was an emotional cripple or demand excellence of me. He'd just love me because I was his mother. In the beginning, my scars quieted themselves. I was a mommy now. For the first time since school, I was good at something. My in-laws were happy. My mother was happy. My husband was happy. Everyone left me alone. But as the child grew, I would have to face my fears again.

When my firstborn was just a toddler, my fear of driving put his little life in danger. One day he climbed out of his crib and up onto a bookcase where I kept some grape-flavored cold medicine. When I found him, his chubby little fingers had managed to open almost a half box of trial-sized bottles. I almost fainted when I saw him swallowing the medication!

I scooped his little body up into my arms, and rushed to call someone to take us to the emergency room because I did not drive. They didn't arrive for another twenty minutes! As I sat on the steps of my apartment building waiting, holding my baby, and crying, I had to face myself again. My fear had not only crippled my own life, but had now endangered the life of my child. The doctor said that because he drank the weaker liquid form of the medicine instead of the stronger syrup, he would be OK. But how easily the story could have had a different ending!

I had obtained my learner's permit years earlier, but had not attempted to take the driver's test until my inability to drive almost cost me my baby. I was so afraid when I finally took the test that I failed. I was so humiliated that I didn't try again for a year—and I failed again. I don't fully understand what frightened me about driving, except that it forced me to make decisions when I was so unsure of myself, and it forced me out into a world that I was desperately afraid of. Eventually though, I passed the test.

My life was still an illusion. My inner life looked nothing like my outer life, which looked full of promise and hope. Both my husband and I had entered the ministry. We'd just moved out of a drug-infested apartment complex into our first home in a nice neighborhood, and had purchased a nice little used car. Life was looking up! But I was crying myself to sleep at night. I felt hopeless and helpless.

I became pregnant with my second child, but even that did not help. I was afraid that my inner drama would affect the child. Before getting pregnant, I was losing the weight that I had been hiding behind for years. Being overweight psychologically protected me from dealing with sexuality any more than was necessary. I was decorating my home; I was determined to pull myself up by my own bootstraps and make something of my life. But at night, I still couldn't sleep.

Though I was molested as a young girl, the emotional scars did not really begin to "show up" until later in life, or at least I did not recognize them as such until I was older. Nightmares and irrational fears of the dark, driving, new things, and of life in general were some of the visible scars. I don't mean nervousness; I mean sickening, paralyzing fear.

I understand better than the average person what John meant when he said, "Fear hath torment. He that feareth is not made perfect in love" (1 John 4:18). I did not love myself and I did not yet understand the love of Christ. I felt constantly overwhelmed by life. It seemed as if the everyday aspects of living were too much for me. The thousand little decisions that need to be made each day and are taken for granted by everyone else seemed to frustrate me beyond belief. I never knew the right thing to do because I did not value my own opinion. And I *so* badly needed to do the right things. In hindsight, I know that I felt responsible for my own abuse and therefore needed to "be good" in order to earn self-worth. I had incredibly low self-esteem, which I covered with my perfectionism.

Perfectionism in itself is torturous because one is never satisfied with oneself, or even with a job done well. One mistake makes you feel as if you are completely stupid and worthless. It erases any pleasure brought by accomplishments or acclaim. Whatever affirmation you receive for your accomplishments is never enough to teach you to love and believe in yourself because you are trying to please an inner voice that is always harsh and destructive.

My battles with depression increased to the point that suicide seemed favorable. I would daydream about it. I grew so tired of life that one day, out of the blue, I told God that I was tired of the way I was living. I told him that I was tired of living a charade; I wanted to be whole through and through, not just on the surface. I told Him that I wanted to be happy like my husband was. Whatever my husband is, he is 100 percent. I gave the Lord permission to do whatever it took to make me whole—even if it hurt. That is the best decision I've ever made. Even though I did not understand the roller coaster ride I was about to get on, if I had known its results I would have made the same decision a thousand times.

Chapter 2

SOUGHT OUT

I WILL NEVER FORGET the first day the Holy Spirit sought me out to deliver me from my hidden scars. He took me at my word and responded *very quickly* to my prayer of anguish and desperation. My husband was out of town on business and I was at home with our young son. I walked in depression even more deeply when my husband was gone because I did not have to hide my shame and loneliness from anyone. So I stumbled through my house, afraid of the phone ringing, and deathly afraid of people coming to visit. I did not feel like bathing or brushing my teeth. I did not feel like cleaning or cooking or going outside to get the mail. I did, however, force myself to go outside to get the mail because I knew that my husband would call and ask about it.

On this particular sunny day, I walked out to the mailbox, and as I turned around to walk back toward the house, the Holy Spirit spoke to me so loudly and clearly that I jumped. He said, "Susan, live!" I answered, "Yes Sir" immediately because of my obedient nature, although I had no idea what He meant.

So trying to comply, I went in the house, opened up all the blinds, turned some jubilant gospel music up loud, and went through the house singing. My immediate reaction was that deliverance, whatever that meant, would come quickly and easily. I was wrong. One of the first things the Holy Spirit said to me was that I had no idea what freedom was because I had never been free. He said, "I must gut you like a fish!" I found out later what He meant. Most of my perceptions about God and life were wrong because they were based on my wounded carnal thinking. He would have to first clean out my erroneous thinking before He could fill me with the truth.

> Strip yourselves of your former nature [put off and discard your old unrenewed self] which characterized your previous manner of life and becomes corrupt through lusts and desires that spring from delusion; And be constantly renewed in the spirit of your mind [having a fresh mental and spiritual attitude].
> —EPHESIANS 4:22–23 AMP

I thought that God was as stern and judgmental with me as I was with myself. I thought He was impatient with my imperfections, an image that I had learned from my relationship with my mother. I must say in her defense, that she did not intend to be intimidating. She drove me toward excellence out of a desire to ensure that my life would never become what hers had. She was a beautiful, intelligent woman, but she felt trapped by poor decisions. She had never believed that she could succeed without a man. Her life choices before salvation were impulsive and self-defeating, for the most part. She acted out of a need for provision and protection for her children. The few real loving relationships she had experienced ended badly.

She intended to produce a strong, self-confident achiever, but because of my scarred childhood (which she did not find out about until I was a grown woman), I learned to be a perfectionist instead. I thought I had to earn love and approval. Therefore, even with God, I considered myself unworthy because of my childhood abuse. My false, religious images of God kept me away from His mercy and healing because I did not know that they were for me. I found out in the course of time, as God began to teach me, who He really is. I discovered that I did not need to be afraid of His rejection, for He had loved and accepted me all along.

I did not know it at the time, but when the Holy Spirit told me to "*Live*," He was referring to a passage of Scripture that I had never read at the time. I did not see the scripture until several months later, when I went to one of the early "Woman Thou Art Loosed" conferences. It was held at an airport hotel in Memphis, Tennessee, where I lived at the time. Bishop Jakes preached from Ezekiel 16. These are the scriptures that seemed to call my name:

> And as for thy nativity, in the day thou wast born thy navel was not cut, neither wast thou washed in water to supple thee; thou wast not salted at all, nor swaddled at all. None eye pitied thee, to do any of these unto thee, to have compassion upon thee; but thou wast cast out in the open field, to the loathing of thy person, in the day that thou wast born. And when I passed by thee, and saw thee polluted in thine own blood, I said unto thee when thou wast in thy blood, Live; yea, I said unto thee when thou wast in thy blood, *Live* (vv. 4–6, emphasis added).

Bishop Jakes went on, but I did not. I was stuck in verse six. All of a sudden everything made sense. Those verses spoke the sentiment of my wounded heart. The abuse had brought me isolation, guilt and self-loathing. Because of it, I felt forsaken, neglected, polluted and so deeply wounded. The Holy Spirit was telling me that God had seen my pain; He had seen the emotional scars. And when He found me in my suffering, He had pity on me and called me to *life*, and that more abundantly!

I'd never felt so loved and so nurtured as when I discovered that God did not require *me* to present to Him a perfect, spotless life on my own. I'm glad, because I did not know how. I thought I had to perform for Him and earn His love as I'd thought I had to earn my mother's. I had accepted Christ at the age of fourteen and had loved God with all my heart since that time, but even that had not made me feel clean of the filth that had traumatized my life. I had to learn that I could bring my wounded, hurting soul and allow Him to make me whole.

Jude 1:24 says:

> Now unto *Him* that is able to keep you from falling, and *to present you faultless* before the presence of his glory with exceeding joy (emphasis added).

The Amplified Version reads:

> Now to Him Who is able to keep you without stumbling or slipping or falling, and to present [you] *unblemished (blameless and faultless)* before the presence of His glory in triumphant joy and exultation [with unspeakable, ecstatic delight] (emphasis added).

I finally got the revelation that it is *Christ* who is able to keep me from falling and that it is *Christ* who is able to present me faultless, not my religious legalism or my perfectionism.

That went against all the religion that I knew. I thought that I had to perform and pretend that all was well in my heart. Even though my spirit was alive, my heart was wounded and broken. I thought that I had to go on helping and praying for others while I hid my own pain, when all I had to do was bring my aching heart to Him just as it was and He would heal me. Before that revelation, I'd never fully understood John 10:10:

> The thief cometh not, but for to steal, and to kill, and to destroy: I am come that they might have life, and that they might have it more abundantly.

I understood the assignment of the thief. That's all the old saints seemed to talk about—what the devil did and how good he was at doing it. I did not understand, however, what "abundant life" was. At first I thought it simply meant eternal life. But the Holy Spirit brought a deeper understanding. This abundant life was more than life after death; it was overflowing and victorious life here on Earth—a full life! Abundant life is so full of the love of God that it spills over and touches everyone around you. This is not only God loving you, but you loving Him back and enjoying your life in and with Him!

Chapter 3

FINALLY LOOKING *for* LOVE *in the* RIGHT PLACE

*M*Y UNDERSTANDING OF true love had been damaged. It was carnal, emotional, and unhealthy. I'd totally identified with the idea of tortured love. But as God continued to reveal Himself to me, my understanding of love grew. Agape love began to make sense. It is a decision to love—a commitment to love without requiring prerequisites or conditions. This revelation helped me to finally accept God's love for me. All my feelings of insufficiency and unworthiness could not override God's choice to love me.

It was the acceptance of His love for me that eventually taught me how to love myself. I did not think I deserved love because I was not perfect. This stronghold in my thinking prevented me from accepting the love of others. I had always been able to give love, but not to fully receive it. I believed that any love offered to me would be taken away as soon as all my hidden scars and flaws began to show through. In the past, no matter who showed me love, I still felt lonely. I thought their love was based on the image I projected and what I could offer in return. Since I did not feel I had much to give in return, I lived in constant expectation of rejection and abandonment.

The sweetness of God's unmerited love for me began to open up my heart. One of my hidden scars was the inability to trust. The Holy Spirit spoke to me one day as I was grappling with the war in my mind, wanting to be loved yet afraid to trust love. *"Susan,"* He said, *"You can have the walls that you have set up to protect yourself if you choose. If you choose them, you will be protected from hurt to a small degree; but you will never experience the depth and type of love that you desire because love always exposes us to vulnerability."* He also said, *"When you have come full circle into complete wholeness and liberty, you will give love because you choose to love, fully accepting the possibility that you may not be loved in return."* This God kind of love does not love because of what it expects to receive, but because of what it desires to give.

Because of what He said, I eventually learned to love and be loved, never knowing what the future would bring but fully committed to give my all each and every day. That forced me to learn to trust God and man. I am not foolish, I know that not everyone is honest and well intentioned—but I no longer give love in order to earn love. I give love now because I want to give it. I give love because I feel like a prisoner who's been set free. I am so loved that I would burst if I did not give it out to others. I have had the flip side—locked up, lonely, and miserable. I'd rather live big, open, and joyfully, getting hurt at times, but going on to experience life and that more abundantly!

Since I have begun this love walk, I have been hurt deeply. People I thought were friends have betrayed me. I have been lied on by people to whom I exposed my heart. I have been attacked by people who somehow perceived me as a threat to them. Each time, the enemy offers me the opportunity to shut down and shut everyone else out again. But when I remember how miserable life was before I was delivered from the bondage of defining my life by my pain, I make the decision again to love as God loves, freely and purely.

The Holy Spirit has tested my love and found me sorely

lacking many times. It is easy to love the lovable, but we have to allow the Spirit to teach us how to love the unlovable—how to intercede for them, how to look past their behavior and words and discover the source of their pain. Then we must learn to pray for their healing instead of retribution. It is not easy. It does not feel good. But it is what pleases God and brings Him glory. That is what I want to do. Don't you?

Many times I am reminded of the woman in Luke chapter 7. She was "an especially wicked woman" who invited herself to a feast that took place in Simon the Pharisee's house. Sinful, ashamed, and unwelcomed, she made herself a place at Jesus' feet and wept so deeply that her tears began to wet His feet. She took her long hair and wiped them dry. Then she broke her alabaster box of ointment and anointed Jesus' feet. Jesus did not say a word. Simon the Pharisee, the owner of the house, questioned the holiness and anointing of Jesus for allowing such a woman to caress Him so. In rebuke to the Pharisee, Jesus simply told him a story about two debtors. One owed little, one owed much. Since neither could pay, the creditor forgave both their debts. Jesus asked the Pharisee, "*Which of them will love the creditor most?*" The Pharisee rightly answered, "*I suppose the one whom he forgave and cancelled more.*" Jesus emphasized the fact that since He had entered the Pharisee's house, Simon had done nothing to show Him love and hospitality, but the sinful woman had not ceased to kiss and anoint Jesus' feet since He arrived. Jesus then made this statement:

> Therefore I tell you, her sins, many [as they are], are forgiven her—because she has loved much. But he who is forgiven little loves little (v. 47, AMP).

He then spoke to the woman directly and said, "Your sins are forgiven!" This story makes me cry. I identify so much with this woman. My hidden scars made me feel so unclean and so unworthy. Yet when I consider how unworthy I felt and how greatly He loves me, my only response can be to love Him in return.

I have no desirable pedigree. I come from a family of unwed mothers and adulterers, alcoholics and drug addicts, and everything else you can name. We were not rich or powerful or great in any way except in sin. Most of my sisters were repeatedly molested as I was, as if we had no worth or feelings. But the unconditional love of God found us, and gave us hope and a future with meaning and purpose. Most of my sisters are in ministry today. They are anointed and making a difference in this world, each having made a choice to give because Christ gave so much to her. Most of my mother's ten children—seven girls and three boys—have accepted Christ as Savior. And those few who have not, will. That is my confession and my belief!

We are all very different, having come from so many different fathers. But the one thing we have in common is that we all love powerfully, because so much debt has been cancelled in our favor. Our God is awesome!

Chapter 4

ISSUES *as* IDOLS

O NE DAY AS I was having a "pity party" and complaining to God about hurtful things that people had said to me, God stopped me and said, "You have made idols of those people." My reaction was religious. The only image that came to my mind was of myself kneeling and worshiping before false gods. I told God, "No! I have not made them idols. You are the only God I worship!"

He said to me, "Whatever I say to you, you dismiss as trivial. I tell you I love you. I tell you that you are fearfully and wonderfully made. I tell you that I have thoughts and plans for you. You respond emotionally, but you soon afterward dismiss those words as if they were only flattery. But whatever someone says to hurt you, you rehearse those words in your mind over and over. You meditate on them at night before you go to sleep. You repeat to others what was said. You have elevated them to the status of idols because you magnify their words and belittle Mine."

All I could do was cry. I had not seen what I was doing. His truth began to make me free. I responded passionately, "Lord, take away every idol in my life." His response to me was, "No. You cast them down."

When you don't love yourself, every compliment you receive is easily dismissed as insincere kindness. Even when God is the One who gives the affirmation, your established habit of dismissing kindness as mere politeness continues. The difference that we do not understand is that whatever God speaks of us is truth! His words are Spirit and Life. That is vastly different from a fleshy compliment! When you have made idols of your issues though, their familiarity can become oddly comfortable. Even though you hate the routine, you know it and find it hard to walk away from. *Webster's* dictionary defines *issue* as "emergence; offspring; something coming forth from a specific source; to be a consequence of or descend from a specific parent or ancestor; also to flow out or come or go out." For our purposes we can understand then how our emotional wounds, irrational behaviors and fears came to be popularly called our "issues." They *emerged* from something in our past; they are *consequences* of some poor decision, violation, or loss from our past. We may not always know the exact source of each issue, we just know it's there because we have tracked its pattern in our lives again and again. We become so familiar with the pattern that we claim ownership of those issues. It is entirely possible to find the issues desirable, because we feel that they excuse us from being responsible for our own behavior and attitudes.

HOW AN "ISSUE" IS BORN

Perhaps when someone hurts your feelings, you do not say anything in response. You don't even tell her that she hurt you, but you can't stop thinking about it. You nurse it and rehearse it until the anger and hurt seem to control you. It fills your every waking thought until you birth an "issue" (remember one of the definitions of *issue* is "to give birth" or "offspring"). Now unforgiveness is birthed, and offense follows. Then resentment sets up, soon to be followed by hatred. Some of the hatred is turned inward because you are angry with yourself for not having the courage to speak up.

You develop a hatred for the individual who hurt you when the offender may not even be aware that she hurt you. Your hatred allows you to be jealous of every success or gain she makes. You may try to sabotage the person's success, or at least destroy her reputation by spreading gossip. It does not even have to be true. Your obsession with your hurt feelings can gain such momentum that it takes on details that never existed. By the time you finish the story, she is a monster and you are the poor, innocent victim. Now you have no time to work toward your own advancement or success because all your energy is expended in destroying hers.

That is just one scenario. Issues become idols when your entire life is judged and measured by them—when every person and every situation is colored through the dimly lit glasses of your "issue." When you reject the Word of God because you don't believe you can overcome, or don't want to overcome your "issue"—it has definitely become an idol. When you reject healing and deliverance—when you refuse your destiny because you refuse to give up your right to your "issue"—it has become your idol, and you cannot move forward until you cast it down.

Chapter 5

FROM BABY STEPS
to GIANT STEPS

THE STEPS TO deliverance were given to me in hindsight. I first experienced them unaware of any symmetry or order. I just kept my ears and heart open daily and followed the leading of the Holy Spirit as closely as I could. I did not know to treasure what I was being taught as I do now. I did not write down everything that happened; I was chastened for that later. But thank God for His mercy in helping me to remember it through the power of the Holy Spirit bringing it back to me. These steps are, in a nutshell, what happened to me over the course of several years.

STEPS OF DELIVERANCE

Illumination

This is the unveiling of the scars. Find out the source of your scars and identify the lies and erroneous thinking that you have "bought into" as a result of them. Jesus showed me the roots of my wrong thinking. The Holy Spirit showed me when and where my unhealthy thinking started—then replaced it with His truth.

And ye shall know the truth, and the truth shall make you free.

—JOHN 8:32

A few days after the Holy Spirit promised that He would heal and deliver me, I began to experience flashbacks, remembering minute details of my sad childhood. This disturbed me because it brought me great pain to remember things that had been suppressed so long. I thought something was wrong; this could not be the work of a loving Savior. When I asked the Lord about it, He told me that I needed to confront and deal with the emotions and pain that I had been unable to face as a child. He said that emotions had been given to help us deal with life, but not to rule us. If suppressed, these memories do not disappear, they merely internalize and fester. They show up as emotional or mental problems, or even health problems. Therefore, I had to take the time to face the memories and let out the emotions that I had bottled up because I was unable to deal with them.

It was a slow, painful process. I had to stay committed to the healing process in order to resist the temptation to give up. It is at times easier to revert to our past way of thinking and behaving, even if we did not care for it, because the familiar, painful past can feel safer than the unknown path before us. I had to remember the terrible emotional chains I had been bound with in order to remind myself to keep pressing for a better future. Though the future was unknown and frightening because it required so much change on my part, I knew it had to hold more promise than the past from which I had come.

This part of the process not only unveiled past memories and suppressed emotions; the Lord also showed me what had produced my scars (fear, self-hatred, and perfectionism, among other things).

Acknowledgment

There can be no distinction between lies and the truth unless you first know which is which. In this stage you have to begin embracing God's truth over your own feelings, opinions, and traditions, and determining which is which. It is a bold step to reject what you've always known to embrace what is new and strange to you. In the past, I had allowed my feelings to run my life. So through manipulating them, Satan kept me in bondage. I was born again, my spirit was brand new, but my mind still needed to be renewed!

You must also acknowledge your part in the existence or progression of your scars. You may not be responsible for what happened to you as a child, but you are responsible for the choices you have made as an adult. Taking responsibility for our actions helps us understand that it is our responsibility to change them.

During this period I began my part of the process. I researched God's Word to determine the truth in areas where I had previously made my own opinions. The Holy Spirit taught me that it was my responsibility to acknowledge my wrong opinions and choices and to confess God's Word instead. I had to "put off the old man" (Eph. 4:22; Col. 3:9). It took conscious effort to stop thinking, speaking, and behaving in my old ways. Those ways had brought me depression and bondage.

Changing what you've thought and spoken all your life is not an overnight process. But there is no other option if you want God's freedom. I made frequent slip-ups in the beginning. The Holy Spirit would correct and teach me each day until I finally began to change my speech. Even when I did, my emotions did not immediately line up with God's truth. For example, it was not easy to confess that I was "fearfully and wonderfully made" (Ps. 139:14) when I felt like such an ugly ducking, but I spoke it because it was God's Word.

As I continued to be obedient, eventually my emotions began to agree with God's Word. I still had to resist the devil, but as God's Word began to win out I started to change—in thought, in word, and in deed. The change was so powerful that people around me began to notice. I began to feel good, and even look better!

Meditation/Recognition

In this stage, you begin to recognize how the scar operates in your daily life; its characteristics, its attitudes, and its self-defeating triggers.

I remember asking God why He couldn't simply take all of this ugliness out at one time. He answered, "I could, but you could not handle it." I realize now that it takes time to renew the mind. So each time I gloated in my early victories, thinking that the deliverance process was almost finished, new things would come up, and I would find myself at the beginning again.

I thought that I was failing until the Holy Spirit taught me that I was actually advancing. Sometimes in a race there are periodic hurdles to jump. In hindsight, I understand this so much better. The stretches between the hurdles became much longer once I began to run the race and apply the lessons that I had learned. Hurdles still confront me, but His grace and truth lead me safely over them.

To know that you have a scar is not deliverance. To understand how that scar defeats you is not deliverance. But to know how to take that scar to Christ and allow Him to destroy its power in your life—that is deliverance. Deliverance does not take away the memory of your wounded past, but it renders your past ineffective at ruining the rest of your life. If we are not very careful, this generation will miss the powerful deliverance that obedience brings because it has been bombarded by a media and society that teaches that we have no responsibility for who we are or for what we do. That is a powerful deceiver because it steals from us the power to change. When we assign blame to others, we are confessing that others have more power over our lives than we do.

People run from church to church and from conference to conference searching for deliverance. We can be prayed for, taught principles, and encouraged by others, but I believe the true work of deliverance can only be done by the Holy Spirit working in and with us. I don't believe deliverance can be experienced without our obedience and submission to the Word that we already know. We all seem to be looking for some new magical truth that will make all trouble go away without any effort of self-denial on our part. That is not the way of true growth. Christ transforms us by our faith in and obedience to His Word, not by mysticism and goose bumps.

Revelation/God's Truth Revealed

According to Webster's dictionary, to *know* means to perceive directly as fact; to experience, to believe to be true, to be certain of.

Replace the lies with God's truth. Allow God's Word to rule and replace your old negative thoughts and confessions. Speak God's truth out loud. Replace your old mind-set with His. Replace your old confessions with His concerning you.

> And you will know the Truth, and the Truth will set you free.
>
> —JOHN 8:32, AMP

The only reason I decided to name this stage separately from the last is because I perceive this to be the point when we begin to *accept* God's truth above our opinions. We are not submitting only out of obedience; we have embraced and experienced His truth above and beyond facts, feelings, or conventional wisdom. When we get here, we have had enough experience with Him to trust Him, whether or not we understand. We have experienced that His way works, and therefore we do it His way.

Determined Decision to Change

Make a decision to let go of the scars and to let the Word of God discipline your life. You must intently, intentionally, purposefully, aggressively, and persistently pursue deliverance! Make whatever changes are necessary. You may even need to remove people from your life who hinder your motivation to change.

There will be overt and subtle sabotage of your press toward abundant life because strongholds that used to control you won't give up without a fight. The battle will be both natural and spiritual. Remember your fight is not against people, but mind-sets and strongholds. Most people won't understand when or why they are trying to sabotage you, and some wouldn't even believe it if you told them.

Casting Down Strongholds

Repetitively and aggressively reject old thought, speech, and behavior patterns with a relevant scripture, prayer, and confession until the old mind-set or stronghold is replaced by God's truth.

(For the weapons of our warfare are not carnal, but mighty through God to the pulling down of strong holds;) Casting down imaginations, and every high thing that exalteth itself against the knowledge of God, and bringing into captivity every thought to the obedience of Christ.

—2 CORINTHIANS 10:4–5

And even then, constantly be renewed in the spirit of your mind by rehearsing the truth on a regular basis.

Live the Truth, Speak the Truth, Do the Truth

Apply everything you have learned daily! The object of every lesson is life application—for the rest of your life. Knowledge of the need to change without application of the means and method of change is useless.

This is where many stall out. They know and discuss what is needed but are too afraid of the change that will be required. To walk in a new lifestyle can be frightening when all you know and see around you supports your old one. Therefore, get yourself around people who support your new walk. If possible, get away from the unsupportive; if not, learn to protect yourself until you can do something different. Remember Joseph. We can't always share our dreams with everyone.

These last several steps happen simultaneously. Your efforts to permanently walk away from allowing the past to rule your present will need to be exercised and reinforced for the rest of your life. Strongholds aren't always cast down without a fight, so you must keep your spiritual armor on. Always be prepared to battle the enemy in your mind, your relationships, and your environment. You may be surprised at the people and circumstances that will resist your change. Do not regard them as the enemy, but be wise enough to stay away from those that tend to sabotage your faith or resolve until you are built up in your most holy faith.

Chapter 6

FRAGMENTED *vs.* WHOLE

Humpty Dumpty sat on a wall
Humpty Dumpty had a great fall
All the king's horses and all the king's men
Couldn't put Humpty together again

I ONCE HEARD THAT Mother Goose's nursery rhymes are more than what they seem on the surface. Many of them were social commentary on political issues hidden in the form of children's rhymes. "Humpty Dumpty" could be considered social commentary on some of our lives. Many of us have encountered great falls from which we were wounded so deeply that we broke into fragments.

A fragment is a part broken off, detached, or incomplete. Emotional or spiritual fragmentation happens when a "part of us" remains connected and focused on the time and place we were wounded. When we try to move forward in our lives we are diminished, weakened, or disabled because "all of us" is not available for the present. That particular emotional wound has left a permanent scar in our subconscious mind. That memory or sentiment is always just beneath the surface, and it affects the way we behave in the present.

For example, sometimes we are afraid to trust now because someone we loved betrayed us or let us down in the past. Or we have trouble with anger because someone hurt us in the

35

past and we didn't resolve our anger then, so it keeps coming up now. Perhaps we are in co-dependent relationships because we are so afraid of being rejected again that we attach ourselves to unworthy relationships (thinking that we deserve no better). Because we are not whole, none of our relationships are healthy and whole. We grieve over those relationships that we should let die, and we toss away those that we need to pursue.

It is very easy to pretend that we are whole until something happens that reminds us of our painful past, and all the fury and shame of our "fragmentation" comes back with multiplied force. The most frequent reaction to our fragmented past is to ignore it, thinking that it will go away. Years pass and life goes on, and we begin to believe that the past does not bother us anymore. But we have no explanation for the depression that keeps nagging at us, or the aggression and anger that is always just beneath the surface. We do not understand the manic mood swings that make us "feel crazy." Most likely, you are not crazy; the fragments of your past just keep breaking off more and more of you until there's hardly any strength left to deal with the present.

> May God himself, the God who makes everything holy and whole, make you holy and whole, put you together— spirit, soul, and body—and keep you fit for the coming of our Master, Jesus Christ.
> —1 THESSALONIANS 5:23, THE MESSAGE

We need spiritual and emotional integration. We need to "gather up the fragments that remain, that nothing be lost," as Jesus said in John 6:12.

In order to function with passion and focus on our destiny, we need all our faculties "front and center." If our mind is spread out all over the place, grieving and stressing over our past, we face the future severely weakened and handicapped. The Lord is more than willing to make us whole. He has already given us everything that pertains to life and godliness. The definition of *whole*, according to Webster's dictionary, is healthy; unhurt; entire; free of wound or injury; mentally or emotionally sound, and complete.

In John chapter five, when Jesus saw the man at the pool of Bethesda, who had been infirmed for thirty-eight years, He was moved with compassion. Jesus asked the man, "Wilt thou be made whole?" (v. 6) or in our words, "Are you really serious about being getting well?"

This man had been lame for a long time. The Lord has a burden for those who feel trapped by their situations because not every trial ends quickly. Not every deliverance is immediate; in fact, deliverance from emotional issues will not take place overnight! But gradual deliverance is no less miraculous, for God is still the Strong Deliverer.

You may feel like you have been fighting this battle for so long that your life will never be different than it is now. Remember that feelings are not fact. The very God of peace can make you whole: mind, soul, and body, completely whole and holy.

Chapter 7

SYMPTOMS *of* HIDDEN SCARS

A CHURCH COUNSELOR ONCE told me an awesome analogy. He compared our emotions to the need to breathe when underwater. Right at the last moment, when one can hold his breath absolutely no longer, he feels as if his heart is about to explode. The counselor explained that our emotions need to breathe too, and if we suppress them, they too will explode! They will hide inside of us until they explode themselves into sickness, rotting teeth, migraines, backaches, or other issues. I thought his analogy was amazing because it reminded me of a lesson that the Holy Spirit had taught me earlier.

When the Holy Spirit began to teach me about being healed, He said, "I gave you emotions to help you process life. They are not to rule your life, but they do need to be acknowledged and expressed." Therefore, I had to go back and deal with the emotions that I had not allowed myself to experience when I was abused or deeply hurt.

Over the years, in my own experience and in talking to others, I have seen certain patterns emerge. I am no expert or authority, so I am sure that there are more hidden scars than I understand, but I will share what I have observed.

Anger

In pastoring, we confront many instances where we must investigate the source of ungodly behavior. I believe that all behavior has a root cause. I have found that a background plagued with childhood abuse is at the root of many negative behaviors, including uncontrollable anger or rage. Many people spew out anger at the world because they have never found peace or closure to a painful past experience. Some transfer their anger to a "safe target," someone they feel that they can intimidate, because they cannot bring themselves to confront the actual person against whom they hold their anger. If they would only take the time to acknowledge the anger and let it out in a controlled, safe way, they could experience major healing.

The Holy Spirit had to remind me of Ephesians 4:26, which teaches us, "Be ye angry and sin not: let not the sun go down upon your wrath." I believed that it was a sin to be angry, because in my southern, African American upbringing, its expression was not allowed. The Holy Spirit taught me that it is not a sin to *feel* anger. Anger must be controlled, but it must also be acknowledged. Borrowing from the analogy of the counselor, we must allow our anger to breathe. How much better off we would be if we immediately acknowledged our anger, gave it a healthy outlet such as prayer or exercise, and then let go of it by sundown.

I believe is all right to express our anger in prayer. God is not fragile. He wants us to be real with Him so that He can help us, instead of pretending and being religious with the One who already sees and knows all.

NEED FOR CONTROL AND SECURITY

Another hidden scar that I have seen evolve from childhood pain is the need to control. If left unchecked, this need can become a controlling spirit. I had developed a tendency to be bossy and controlling, but not because I thought that I had all the answers (which was the reason people thought). Instead, I discovered that being sexually abused had left me with abhorrence of feeling vulnerable. Any kind of social or emotional vulnerability reminded me of how I felt when I was taken advantage of by authority figures. So in order to avoid feeling vulnerable, I tended to take control. Being in control made me feel safer.

This need became an issue in my relationship with God. I had trouble trusting Him and leaving situations in His hand, because in my carnal thinking, God was a male, and men had mostly let me down. I loved God immensely, but had trouble trusting His handling of my life. This caused knee-jerk reactions of resistance when the Holy Spirit prompted me to do things that I was afraid of or felt uncomfortable with. My resistance grieved me greatly, but I felt unable to rest in God's faithfulness and His love.

When my husband and I became pastors, my faith walk was greatly hindered by my need to know and understand everything God was doing. I whined and complained for the first several years, until the Lord had to deal with me. I tried to use my emotional scars to negotiate with God. I said, "Lord you know my background. I just need security!" He only answered, "*I* am your Security!" I will not pretend that I don't fight the urge to require understanding before obedience now and then, but I renew my mind and eventually move on.

Fear

The greatest stronghold of my past was dealing with irrational fear. It had been as debilitating to me as alcohol is to an alcoholic. It developed after I was abused, and it ruled every day of my life until Christ delivered me. I was afraid of life! I was afraid to try new things, afraid to meet new people, afraid to drive; afraid *period.*

My freedom came from the Word of God and learning that faith had to be demonstrated by action. I quoted 2 Timothy 1:7 until I was hoarse. But fear did not begin to be cast down until I learned to step out in faith. The more I obeyed in faith, the more fear was destroyed. To complete an earlier analogy, I now treat fear like a former alcoholic treats liquor. I don't speak it in casual jokes. I don't watch scary movies. I don't read scary books. Fear once had such control over me that it ruled my life, so I treat it as a worthy opponent. I don't dread it, but I don't take it for granted either.

Shame

The spirit of shame is a hidden scar that is seldom recognized. The most confusing thing about a stronghold is that it has held onto us for most of our lives and therefore we don't recognize it is a stronghold until the light of truth enters and dispels the darkness. Some of us at times have been walking in a spirit of shame and have not been made aware of it.

A spirit of shame can express itself in many different ways: poor self-esteem, intimidation, inordinate shyness, a burden of guilt, and co-dependency, to name a few. My shame came as a result of feeling responsible for my own abuse. I thought that something must have been wrong with me for that to happen. As I said before, children tend to take responsibility for what goes wrong around them. Most abused people that I have talked with feel in some way guilty for what happened to them. That is why we hide ourselves from relationships.

Because Scripture declares that the truth will make us free (John 8:32), we must confess the truth: we were not responsible for someone's choice to take advantage of us. When a person makes a conscious choice to sin, someone is injured. We were the injured parties. Accepting Christ's love helped me to cast down the spirit of shame. His Word tells me that I am accepted in the Beloved (Eph. 1:6). He tells me that there is no condemnation to those who are in Christ Jesus (Rom. 8:1). I receive by faith my wholeness in Him.

CONFUSION ABOUT SEXUAL IDENTITY

A very strong pattern that I have encountered, especially in abused males, is confusion about their sexual identity. I have ministered to several young men who loved the Lord greatly but were in bondage to homosexual lifestyles and thoughts, because no one had ever shown them that Christ had already freed them. All of them had been molested as young boys by older males.

First Corinthians 6:16 teaches us that when two people engage in intercourse, they become one. Because their very first sexual stirrings were awakened by someone of the same sex, they desired that type of behavior. Because it was the first experience that they'd ever known, these young people began to accept these thoughts and feelings as their own—when in fact they were not. A spirit had been given an open door and they, being so young, had no idea how to fight it. For males this is especially difficult, because most feel that they can confide in no one. If they do, they are either mocked and stigmatized or seduced by another. This even happens within the church. After the pattern is set, these individuals feel trapped into acting out their desires.

The church must accept some responsibility for the perpetuation of this vicious pattern. Either we pretend not to see the problem and avoid it completely, or we attack the person instead of confronting the sin. All sin is equal to God, yet we treat homosexuality as if it is the unpardonable sin. If a subject makes us uncomfortable, we pronounce judgment and dismiss it. We are losing a lot of potentially great men and women because we refuse to confront the hard issues with the love and power of Christ.

We must offer Christ to those trapped by homosexuality and offer them the same patience and compassion as we would an alcoholic or a person dealing with addiction. The gospel of Jesus Christ is the power of God unto salvation for everyone that believeth (Rom. 1:16). We cannot ignore a problem that has crept into our schools, our churches, and even our homes. We must have faith that the same Christ who delivered us can also deliver anyone else. I have seen several young men delivered and set free from the bondage of homosexual sin. They manifest the glory of God by reminding us all what Christ can do with a broken life.

Many of the sexual issues we see in modern society are directly related to childhood molestation. Our pain sends us running for places to hide. Some hide in promiscuity. Some hide in frigidity. Some hide in deviant lifestyles such as pornography, prostitution, or a life of crime.

❧

I do not have a quick, easy answer for all of the world's ills. But I do know who the answer is—Christ. I must say that accepting Christ as Savior does not make all of our problems disappear automatically. We are born again immediately, but it takes time to renew our minds and thereby change our behavior, to walk in real holiness of lifestyle and speech. I believe that in some ways, we see immediate change when we accept Christ. But I have also seen many people struggle in their walk with God because they were never taught that some strongholds must be dealt with on a deeper level. Maturity takes time.

In the church we tend to hide our scars instead of learning to take them to Christ, and thereby perpetuate hypocrisy and shame. Why should we pretend to be free when we can be free indeed? Jesus said, *"Come unto me, all ye that labor and are heavy laden, and I will give you rest. Take my yoke upon you, and learn of me; for I am meek and lowly in heart: and ye shall find rest unto your souls. For my yoke is easy, and my burden is light"* (Matt. 11:28–30). We have to learn to exchange our yoke for His. The anointed One is our yoke destroyer.

I can only speak the things that I have seen, and testify of those things that I have heard. I know what Christ did in me. I was changed from a woman who was dying inside from hidden scars, to one who is experiencing life, and that more abundantly. God is no respecter of persons. What He did for me, He will do for you—if you just ask. He will heal your hidden scars and give you a life of fullness that will bring Him glory. One of my best friends coined a phrase that I have never forgotten. She said, "The power of the gospel is a transformed life!" All I can say to that is, "Amen!"

ABOUT *the* AUTHOR

Susan Woods Rodgers is co-pastor of Fullness of Joy Ministries Inc. and the first lady of New Dimensions Ministries. She serves as Director of Empowering Women Ministries, and host of the Empowering Women Conference.

Susan feels a passionate call to help hurting men and women find the empowerment and abundant life that she found through the power of the Word and discover healing through God's love.

Susan is happily married to Adrian R. Rodgers, pastor of Fullness of Joy and New Dimensions Ministries. They are fulfilling both a calling and a dream by serving together in ministry. Susan and Adrian have one son, Adrian Charles, and one daughter, Brianna Danielle, who are also active in ministry.

You can find out more about Susan on their ministry websites, fojministries.org and newdministries.org.

CONTACT *the* AUTHOR

WEBSITES:

fojministries.org

and

newdministries.org